THE PACER FAMILY

THE PACER FAMILY

END OF AN ERA

Fred Kerr

PEN & SWORD
TRANSPORT

First published in Great Britain in 2018 by
Pen & Sword Transport
An imprint of
Pen & Sword Books Ltd
47 Church Street
Barnsley
South Yorkshire
S70 2AS

Copyright © Fred Kerr 2018

ISBN 978 1 52672 693 3

A CIP catalogue record for this book is
available from the British Library.

Typeset in 11pt Minion by Mac Style Ltd, Bridlington, East Yorkshire
Printed and bound in India by Replika Press Pvt Ltd

Pen & Sword Books Limited incorporates the imprints of Atlas, Archaeology, Aviation, Discovery, Family History,
Fiction, History, Maritime, Military, Military Classics, Politics, Select, Transport, True Crime, Air World,
Frontline Publishing, Leo Cooper, Remember When, Seaforth Publishing, The Praetorian Press,
Wharncliffe Local History, Wharncliffe Transport, Wharncliffe True Crime and White Owl.

For a complete list of Pen & Sword titles please contact
PEN & SWORD BOOKS LIMITED
47 Church Street, Barnsley, South Yorkshire, S70 2AS, England
E-mail: enquiries@pen-and-sword.co.uk
Website: www.pen-and-sword.co.uk

Front Cover: Class 142 142031 passes New Lane on 2 November 2007 whilst working a Southport–Rochdale service.

Rear Cover: 142049 stands at Ormskirk 'interchange' on 10 April 2013 as Class 507 trainset 507033 *Councillor Jack Spriggs* waits to continue to Liverpool; the once through line is now divided by a buffer stop between the two trainsets that is seen in front of 142049.

Contents

Section 1: Prototype Vehicles...8

1.1: LEV1 – Leyland Evaluation Vehicle 1 8

1.2: LEV2 – Leyland Evaluation Vehicle 2 9

1.3: RB002 – Railbus 002 9

1.4: RB003 – Railbus 003 9

1.5: RB004 – Railbus 004 9

1.6: Class 140...9

Section 2: Class 141 11

Section 3: Class 142 14

3.1: Provincial Railways *[4 January 1982 to 3 April 1989]* 14

3.2: Regional Railways *[4 April 1989 to 31 March 1997]* 27

3.3: Privatisation 47

Section 4: Class 143 92

4.1: Provincial Railways *[1982 to 3 April 1989]* later Regional Railways *[4 April 1989 to 31 March 1997]*.................92

4.2: Arriva Trains Wales *[8 December 2003 to 31 March 2018]* 94

4.3: Wessex Trains *[October 2001 to 31 March 2006]* 98

4.4: First Great Western [FGW] *[1 April 2006 to 31 March 2019]* later re-branded Great Western Railways [GWR] *[20 September 2015 to 31 March 2019]* 101

Section 5: Class 144 102

5.1: Provincial Railways *[1982 to 3 April 1989]* 102

5.2: Regional Railways *[4 April 1989 to 1 March 1997]* 103

5.3: Merseyside Travel Ltd (MTL) *[2 March 1997 to 17 February 2000]* 107

5.4: Arriva Trains North *[17 February 2000 to 11 December 2004]* 108

5.5: Northern Rail (NR) *[12 December 2004 to 31 March 2016]* 113

The 'Pacer' story began in 1977 when British Railways (BR) sought a cheap replacement for its ageing Diesel Multiple Unit (DMU) fleet and its Derby-based Research Unit trialled, among other options, the combination of a Leyland bus body bonded to a 4-wheel freight vehicle chassis.

Various prototypes were produced leading to an initial order being placed in 1983 for twenty 2-car units, designated Class 141, to be operated by the West Yorkshire Passenger Transport Executive (WYPTE). The trainsets were powered by a Leyland T11 engine, rated at 200 hp/152 kW, located under each vehicle driving through a Self Changing Gears (SCG) Mechanical Gearbox. Operating experience led to orders for improved designs being placed in 1984 with Derby Works (Class 142), Andrew Barclay (Class 143) and Derby Works (Class 144). The original coupling equipment fitted to the Class 141 fleet was altered for these later orders and, in 1988, all twenty Class 141 trainsets were upgraded with the later couplings by Andrew Barclay, enabling them to work in multiple with Classes 142/143/144. The 'Pacer' trainsets were intended to operate on branch line services but over time both their area of operation and the nature of their services changed, as illustrated in this album.

When introduced, both the Leyland engine and SCG gearbox proved troublesome hence 142050 was built with a Voith 4-speed epicyclic gearbox/cardan shaft combination that was trialled before the decision was taken to replace the Leyland engine with a more powerful Cummins engine and the SCG gearboxes with the Voith transmission on all the Class 14x vehicles during the 1990s. This initially led to the decision to renumber the trainsets as they were modified but this change was applied to Class 143 vehicles only.

As this book was being prepared during 2017, the future of the 'Pacer' family was uncertain as new franchises were being negotiated that called for the withdrawal of 'Pacer' trainsets from Network services by 2020. While valued by the operators because of their cheapness to run, they were unpopular with passengers because of their basic design and were set to cost a great deal to upgrade in order to meet the new legislative requirements of the Rail Vehicle Accessibility (Interoperable Rail System) Regulations 2008. These required the provision of toilets for handicapped passengers and improvements to accessibility by handicapped passengers including those in wheelchairs. Despite the criticisms, however, the 'Pacer' trainsets have been operated for over thirty years and proved to be a reliable – if uncomfortable – trainset that has provided services that might otherwise have been withdrawn had more expensive trainsets been operated.

This album is a tribute to both the wide variety of services operated by the trainsets as well as showing the numerous operators that have used them during the many changes that have taken place since their introduction; this not only includes the re-organisation of the Passenger Transport Executives (PTEs) which initially operated them but also the post-privatisation era when numerous franchises have also operated them on their services.

@ Fred Kerr April 2018

Preserved prototype vehicle Leyland Evaluation Vehicle 1 (LEV1) stands in the Sheringham yard of the North Norfolk Railway (NNR) on 16 August 2004.

Section 1:
Prototype Vehicles

1.1: LEV1 – Leyland Evaluation Vehicle 1

The venture began in 1977 when BR's Derby-based Research Centre and British Leyland joined forces to investigate lightweight vehicle technology, based on the combination of a BR 2-axle chassis supporting a Leyland National bus-body. The Leyland vehicle was chosen because it was produced in modular form by a modern plant at Workington thus allowing vehicles of different length to be provided.

Initially the vehicle was unpowered and was towed at speeds of up to 80 mph coupled between two coaches in order to check ride quality, suspension performance and internal noise levels. The tests began in June 1978 and ran on the WCML to Carlisle following which the vehicle returned to Derby for the fitment of a drive train. The vehicle became identified as Leyland Evaluation Vehicle No 1 (LEV1), bearing Departmental number of RDB 975874, with a drive train comprising an under-floor Leyland 510 engine (rated at 200 hp/152 kW) coupled to a Self Changing Gears (SCG) mechanical gearbox. At the same time, LEV1 was fitted with a bulbous fairing above the cab windows, removal of doors at one end of the unit and the fitting of mesh grilles to the bus-type windscreens.

The vehicle was released for trails in June 1980, with a break for a visit to the USA in 1980 for evaluation, and when they were completed its importance to Railbus development led to it entering preservation with the National Rail Museum (NRM); after a period of storage it moved to the North Norfolk Railway in June 2004 on long-term loan and where its restoration to working order began; in 2012 it was moved to Shildon where, as at December 2016 it is on display.

A close-up view of the bulbous front addition above the cab windscreen and the coupling surround.

LEV1 stands in Sheringham station yard on 16 August 2004 whilst awaiting a start to its lengthy restoration to working order.

1.2: LEV2 – Leyland Evaluation Vehicle 2

LEV2 was produced in response to an order from the USA Department of Transportation following the visit of LEV1. It used a chassis assembled by D. Wickham & Company, based in Ware, and was fitted with a Leyland 690 engine rated at 220 hp. It was completed in August 1981 and, following trials on the Old Dalby test track, was shipped to the USA where it formed part of that country's energy efficiency programme initiated by then President Jimmy Carter.

Following an accident in which the vehicle's light weight – and consequent inability to activate the signalling systems of some companies – came under scrutiny, the trial was abandoned and the vehicle passed into 'preservation' during 1986 since when it has passed through many ownerships. As at December 2016 the vehicle is in the custody of the Connecticut Trolley Museum.

1.3: RB002 – Railbus 002

In 1984 Derby built a single vehicle as a demonstrator which was based on the Class 141 design that had recently been ordered. Initially sent to Denmark in May 1984 it continued onto Sweden before returning to the UK under its own power, including being displayed in Essen (Germany) and Bruges (Belgium) during June 1985. On its return it was modified to Canadian Railway specifications and sent there as a demonstrator; no orders were forthcoming and the vehicle returned to the UK during 1992 and subsequently languished as 'office accommodation' until bought by an Irish millionaire in 1999. The proposed line which it was bought to operate on seems to have been abandoned and, as at December 2016, the vehicle languishes and deteriorates at the site in Riverside Mills adjacent to the Dundalk–Greenore road.

1.4: RB003 – Railbus 003

RB003 was a further stage of development powered by a Leyland T11 engine driven through an SCG R14 gearbox but it still remained conceptually as a single vehicle with no consideration of multiple operation; its basic drawgear was fitted only to allow for haulage in cases of failure. The vehicle was released as an exhibit at the International Union of Public Transport exhibition in Dublin in May 1981 before returning to the UK for further trials at the Old Dalby test track.

The initial trials with BR began on the Western Region in October 1981 but continued on the freight-only Pye Bridge–Worksop line during 1982, during which time it received the Departmental number RDB 977020. In 1982 it was sold to Northern Ireland Railways (NIR) hence requiring re-gauging to the NIR 5 ft 3 in gauge. It was used on the Portrush–Coleraine branch line but criticisms of its poor riding qualities – especially over jointed track – and its inability to cope with increasing demand saw it being withdrawn from service in 1990. It was initially displayed in the Ulster Folk & Transport Museum in Cultra before being moved to the Downpatrick & County Down Railway where it is still located as at December 2016.

1.5: RB004 – Railbus 004

In addition to the RB002 Railbus, Derby produced a version that was moved to the USA in July 1984. After spending two months on trial with the Old Colonial Railroad in Newport it toured railways in both the USA and Canada before returning to the UK during 1986. It moved from Derby Works to ABB Yorks Works for use as a static office. It was sold to the Embsay & Bolton Abbey Railway in August 1994 for restoration but it subsequently passed through many ownerships until being bought by the Railbus Trust in 2011. As at December 2016 the vehicle is based at the Waverley Route Heritage Centre where it provides the site's shuttle service.

1.6: Class 140

While the single Railbus vehicles were being trialled, the BR Business Sectors were sufficiently impressed to consider a 2-car trainset, using the Railbus technology, to cater for services on rural and branch lines, hence funding was provided to build the 2-car trainset that later became designated Class 140. The 2-car trainset was greatly modified from the single vehicle concept with the inclusion of a gangway connection and non-standard cab-ends that met current end-loading requirements; the result was a heavier vehicle at greater cost which moved further away from, rather than nearer to, the lightweight vehicle concept.

The trainset was released to service in 1981 with early trials taking place on routes within the West Yorkshire Passenger Transport Executive (WYPTE) area – centred on Leeds – but was later trialled around the country until returning to Neville Hill depot where it found use as a driver training vehicle. It was sold into preservation with the Keith & Dufftown Railway in 1994 and, as at December 2016, it is slowly being restored to operational use.

Above: RB004 works the shuttle service at the Telford Steam Railway, based in Horsehay, on 28 May 2006.

Right: 140001 finds use as a exhibit at Dufftown (Keith & Dufftown Railway) on 7 March 2004 whilst awaiting restoration to working order.

Section 2:
Class 141

The first order for a 'Pacer' trainset came from BR in 1984 with an order for twenty 2-car units sponsored by the West Yorkshire Passenger Transport Executive (WYPTE) numbered 141.001–020. They were initially operated in WYPTE's Verona Green and Buttermilk livery but, following the introduction of later classes 142–144 with different coupling arrangements, the new coupling was retrofitted when the trainsets were modified by Hunslet-Barclay during 1988–89. At the same time they were renumbered to 141.1xx and re-liveried in WYPTE's then current Red and Cream livery with Metro branding.

This class of 'Pacer' trainset proved troublesome to operate and all trainsets were withdrawn by 1997 when later Class 14x variants became available. Surprisingly 14 units were exported, with 12 being sold to Iran and 2 to the Netherlands, but 4 trainsets (141103/08/10/13) entered preservation within the UK and, as at December 2016, can still be seen at work on heritage lines.

Right: The early trainsets had their bodies delivered from Leyland's Workington plant in Workington Blue livery which was retained whilst the trainset was being built. On 29 January 1984 trainset 141002 bears the blue livery as it passes Corby North whilst on its Derby CW–Bedford Acceptance Run.

Below: The units were initially operated on Leeds–Harrogate–York services as on 29 March 1986 when 141008 was noted passing Poppleton on a York–Leeds service bearing original WYPTE Verona Green and Buttermilk livery.

141107 awaits departure from York on 27 August 1994 with a service to Scarborough.

141108 lies in store at Dereham (Mid-Norfolk Railway) on 19 August 2004 awaiting restoration.

141113 stands in Carrog (Llangollen Railway) on 24 June 2012 awaiting departure with a service to Llangollen whilst operating as a 'guest' visitor during a gala event.

141113 undergoes maintenance in Wolsingham depot (Weardale Railway) on 13 September 2011.

141103 passes Holebeck (Weardale Railway) on 13 September 2011 with a Stanhope–Bishop Auckland service.

Section 3:
Class 142

The Class 142 fleet was the largest of the Pacer classes with 96 trainsets that were ordered in two tranches; 50 trainsets (142001–050) were initially classified Class 142/0 and ordered in January 1984 with delivery to Provincial Railways beginning in June 1985 and a second order, initially classified Class 142/1, was placed in October 1985 for a further 46 trainsets (142051–096) with delivery to Provincial Railways beginning in October 1986; the sub-grouping was soon dispensed with and the trainsets simply identified as Class 142. The vehicles were built in two portions; the bus bodies were built by Leyland Buses at its Workington site then transferred by road to British Rail Engineering's Derby Works where they were secured to a 4-wheel chassis. Two chassis were then coupled together to form a two-car trainset.

The delivery of Class 142/0 trainsets was made in three tranches:

- 142001–142014 to Newton Heath depot for local Manchester services; the units were sponsored by Greater Manchester Passenger Transport Executive (GMPTE) hence carried GMPTE orange/brown livery and intended for GMPTE-sponsored services.
- 142015–142027 to Laira depot for branch line services in Devon and Cornwall.

- 142028–142050 to Newton Heath for local services in Lancashire with the exception of 142049/50 which were delayed; 142049 was sent to the Expo 86 exhibition in Canada with a view to possible orders and 142050 was fitted with a Voith hydraulic transmission to compare with the SCG mechanical transmission.

The delivery of Class 142/1 trainsets was made in two tranches:

- 142051–142070 to Newton Heath for local services in the North West of England.
- 142071–142096 to Neville Hill for local services in West Yorkshire area around Leeds.

3.1: Provincial Railways *[4 January 1982 to 3 April 1989]*

Provincial Railways had been created in January 1982 when train services, including passenger services, of British Rail were divided into sectors as a prelude to privatisation which was created under the Railways Act 1993 and came into effect on 1 April 1994. Provincial Railways operated the local train services – a role that was clarified in April 1989 when the sector was re-named Regional Railways. The sector lasted until 31 March 1997 when the four franchises created under privatisation had begun operating.

A mix of Pacer liveries is displayed at Liverpool Lime St on 13 July 1995 when 142010 in Regional Railways livery with GMPTE branding; 142027 in unbranded chocolate and cream livery and 142043 in Provincial Railways livery with Network North West branding stand at their platforms awaiting their next duty.

3.1.1: GMPTE Sponsored

Trainsets 142001–14 were delivered to Newton Heath depot bearing the GMPTE Orange/Brown livery and GMPTE branding in addition to the BR logo and intended for operation on GMPTE-sponsored services. The western limit of this area was at Wigan but many services from Manchester continued to Southport, where these trainsets became a common sight.

Left: Wigan drivers began driver training in August 1986 and, after classroom work, continued with practical experience between Wigan and Southport. On 7 August 1986 142003 was the trainer trainset, noted in Southport's abandoned excursion siding as the drivers were shown around the paired vehicles.

Below Left: Wigan drivers began driver training in August 1986 and, after classroom work, continued with practical experience between Wigan and Southport. On 5 August 1986 142014 was the trainer trainset, noted in Southport's abandoned excursion siding as the drivers were shown around the paired vehicles.

Below Right: 142014 climbs away from Meols Cop on 28 January 1990 with a Southport–Manchester Victoria service.

142008 + 142028 (bearing Provincial Railways livery) climb away from Meols Cop on 23 July 1989 whilst working a Southport–Manchester Victoria service.

142002 approaches Edge Hill on 8 April 1991 whilst working a Warrington Central–Liverpool Lime St service.

The conversion of Southport steam shed into the Steamport heritage site saw a close relationship being developed between the museum and the local (Liverpool) Area Manager. This resulted in a number of joint exhibitions being held at Southport station during the 1980s with rolling stock from both BR and Steamport being displayed in Southport station. A complementary shuttle service was occasionally operated between the station and Steamport's platform via the connecting line between the two operations.

On 29 August 1986 a joint exhibition was held at Southport and 142002 was provided by BR to provide the shuttle service.

Above: 142002 approaches the Steamport/BR boundary with a Steamport–Southport shuttle service.

Left: 142002 approaches the BR/Steamport boundary with a Southport–Steamport shuttle service.

3.1.2: Cornish Skippers

Trainsets 142015–142027 were allocated to Laira where, as their new role was on the GWR (Great Western Railway) branch lines, they were delivered in May 1986 with the Great Western chocolate and cream livery and promoted locally as 'Skipper' trainsets. The new trainsets, however, proved unsuited to the task due to their lengthy and rigid wheelbase being operated over sharply curved routes hence were quickly replaced, initially by the first generation trainsets they had replaced then by Class 150/2 trainsets with bogies better able to cope with the sharp curves of the Cornish branch lines. The thirteen trainsets had proved to be unlucky in more ways than one and between 1988 and 1989 they were transferred north to be shared between Newton Heath and Neville Hill depots.

142022 curves across Cockwood Harbour on 20 August 1986 whilst working an Exmouth–Paignton service.

142017 crosses Leven Viaduct on 9 June 1990 whilst working a Barrow–Preston service.

142027 climbs away from Meols Cop on 20 November 1988 whilst working a Southport–Manchester Victoria service.

142015 pilots 142044 (bearing Provincial Railways two-tone blue livery with white stripe) out of Meols Cop on 21 May 1988 whilst working a Southport–Manchester Victoria service.

142027 approaches Edge Hill on 4 July 1991 whilst working a Warrington Central–Liverpool Lime St service.

3.1.3: Provincial Railways

Trainsets 142028–49 were delivered to Newton Heath depot bearing Provincial Railways two-tone blue livery with white stripe for use on local services in the Lancashire area. These were quickly followed by 142051–96 which were initially shared between Newton Heath depot (142051–070) for services in the North West of England and Neville Hill depot (142071–96) for local services in the Leeds area.

Above: 142067 curves through Deganwy on 22 July 1992 with a Manchester Victoria–Llandudno service.

Left: 142064 leads a Blackpool North–Manchester Victoria service, comprising 142026 and Class 150/2 150241, through Euxton Junction on 21 May 1988.

142062 curves past Chinley East on 24 October 1987 with a Manchester Piccadilly–Sheffield service.

Left: 142028 departs from Bidston on 30 September 1985 with a Bidston–Wrexham Central service.

Below Left: 142040 passes Miles Platting on 26 April 1986 with a Rochdale–Manchester Victoria service.

Below Right: 142085 powers through Steeton on 20 March 1995 with a Leeds–Skipton local service.

142055 stands at Rufford on 10 April 1987 whilst working an Ormskirk–Blackpool North service.

3.2: Regional Railways [4 April 1989 to 31 March 1997]

Provincial Railways was renamed in April 1989 to Regional Railways to better identify its role in BR's passenger hierarchy but, in parallel, a further sub-sector named Network North West (NNW) was introduced by BR from 4 April 1989. This sub-sector was sponsored by both GMPTE and Lancashire County Council (LCC) to support rail services in the North West of England but it lasted only a short time before being incorporated back into Regional Railways.

3.2.1: Network North West [NNW]

Initially the NNW trainsets retained the Provincial Railways livery but with the added NNW branding until being subsumed into Regional Railways when many were re-liveried into the revised Regional Railways livery based on the early GMPTE orange/brown livery.

142046 + 142010 climb away from Meols Cop on 5 June 1989 with a Southport–Manchester Victoria service; despite being operated by Network North West (NNW) 142046 has yet to be adorned with its NNW branding.

142038 + 142040 + Class 156 156425 await departure from Blackpool North on 16 August 1992 with a service to Manchester Victoria.

Left: 142049 approaches Edge Hill on 4 July 1991 whilst working a Warrington Central–Liverpool Lime St service.

Below Left: 142056 passes through Edge Hill on 30 August 1991 whilst working a Liverpool Lime St–Warrington Central service.

Below Right: 142061 approaches Edge Hill on 8 April 1991 with a Manchester Victoria–Liverpool Lime St service.

142035 curves round the headland on its approach to Parton on 26 July 1995 whilst working a Carlisle–Barrow service.

142058 plus a Class 150/2 trainset race through Pool Hey on 14 April 1990 whilst working a Southport–Manchester Victoria service.

142060 passes Winwick on 22 July 1995 whilst working a Liverpool Lime St–Chester service.

142056 approaches Rufford on 22 May 1993 whilst working a Preston–Ormskirk service.

142043 climbs away from Meols Cop on 13 June 1992 with a Southport–Manchester Piccadilly service.

142071 approaches Southport on 19 July 1991 with a Manchester Victoria–Southport service comprising Class 150/2 150203 and Class 142/1 142039.

3.2.2: Regional Railways [Revised GMPTE livery]

The Regional Railways operation that began from April 1989, in parallel with the Network North West operation, saw trainsets re-liveried in a modified GMPTE livery of grey lower body, red stripe and white window surrounds. Initially GMPTE branding was restricted to trainsets 142001–013 but Newton Heath subsequently applied both the livery and branding to many of its Class 142 trainsets. In the early days of privatisation the new franchisee (First North Western Trains) retained this livery for a short time until creating its own corporate livery.

142038 leaves Liverpool Lime St on 29 March 2000 with a local service to Wigan North Western.

Left: 142034 stables with Class 156 156425 at Preston platform on 26 November 1999.

Below Left: 142037 retains its Provincial Railways two-tone blue livery with white stripe as it curves through Nethertown on 26 July 1995 with a Lancaster–Carlisle service.

Below Right: 142035 departs from Southport on 13 July 1998 with a Southport–Manchester Victoria service.

The early Newton Heath trainsets to adopt the revised GMPTE livery also carried GMPTE logo and Regional Railways branding as exemplified by:

Left: 142010 curving past Southport Windsor Road on 17 July 1998 whilst working a Southport–Manchester Victoria service.

Above: 142030 stabled at Preston on 20 April 2000.

Below: 142005 stabled at Preston after arriving with a Colne–Preston service on 20 April 2000.

A Class 142/0 + Class 142/1, bearing Merseyrail Yellow livery, depart from St Bees on 26 July 1995 with a Carlisle–Lancaster service.

Right: 142067 eases through Balshaw Lane Junction on 22 April 1999 whilst working a Liverpool Lime St–Blackpool North service.

Below Left: 142013 speeds away from Bamber Bridge on 24 April 1999 after calling with a Blackpool South–Colne service.

Below Right: 142012 curves through Winwick Junction on 22 September 1997 whilst working a Liverpool Lime St–Chester service.

In the mid 1990s GMPTE suspended its funding of Regional Railways services and the newly expanded Manchester Airport took over the funding arrangements but replaced the GMPTE logo with that of Manchester Airport. This lasted only a short time until the GMPTE funding was restored.

Left: A pair of Class 142 trainsets stand in Liverpool Lime St on 13 August 1996 displaying the Manchester Airport logo.

Below Left: Class doyen 142001 displays its Manchester Airport logo on 21 December 1996 as it passes Winwick whilst working a Liverpool Lime St–Chester service.

Below Right: 142067 bears the Manchester Airport logo as it passes Winwick on 21 December 1996 whilst working a Chester–Liverpool Lime St service.

3.2.3: Regional Railways (Revised)

In August 1991 142023 appeared in a revised livery based on that which had been applied to the Provincial Railways Class 15x 'Sprinter' fleet and which was applied to many 'Pacer' trainsets in the months leading up to the 1994 privatisation. This section identifies only those Class 142 trainsets which operated from Newton Heath depot prior to transferring to a franchisee; other 'Pacer' trainsets in this livery will be illustrated within the section dealing with the appropriate franchisee within the Class section.

142023 stands in Southport on 12 August 1991 whilst its fuel and water levels are checked.

Left: 142023 speeds through Salwick on 6 May 2000 whilst working a St Annes–Greenbank service.

Bottom Left: 142033 drifts through Winwick on 31 December 1998 whilst working a Chester–Liverpool Lime St service.

Bottom Right: 142048 curves into Southport on 12 September 1995 whilst working a Manchester Victoria–Southport service.

3.2.4: *Merseyrail*

The Merseyside Passenger Transport Executive (MPTE) evolved into MerseyTravel which oversaw the provision of transport services within the Merseyside area – including rail transport which had three branded services. The Northern and Wirral Lines were self-contained electric services operated by MerseyRail under contract to MerseyTravel whilst the third was City Line, encompassing local services working out of Liverpool Lime St.

In 1993 MerseyTravel sponsored a number of Class 142 trainsets for local workings and Class 150/2 trainsets for longer distance services with eight trainsets (142051–058) being painted into Merseyrail Yellow livery with black stripe, Merseyrail branding and 2+3 seating; intended for local use around Liverpool they were pooled with Newton Heath's 'Pacer' fleet to operate on that depot's diagrams.

In 2000/2001 MerseyTravel arranged to exchange its Class 150 trainsets for a further batch of Class 142 trainsets (142041–049) which it refurbished as for the previous batch but replacing the black stripe with a lighter grey one. This revised livery was subsequently applied to the earlier batch but this only lasted a short time as, when the North West franchise was awarded to Northern Rail from 12 December 2004, the 17 Class 142 Merseyrail trainsets received the new franchisee's livery and were pooled with the company's fleet.

For the sake of continuity all the Merseyrail images, both pre- and post-privatisation have been included in this section.

142051 approaches Liverpool Lime St on 29 March 2000 with a service from Morecambe.

Left: 142053 approaches Preston on 24 June 1999 whilst working a Liverpool Lime St–Blackpool North service.

Below Left: 142057 approaches Leyland on 20 July 2002 whilst working a Lancaster–Liverpool Lime St service.

Below Right: 142054 approaches Stockport on 17 August 2002 whilst working a Manchester Piccadilly–Chester Service.

Right: 142053 curves through Chinley East Junction on 4 May 1995 whilst working a Manchester Piccadilly–Sheffield working.

Below Left: The Rainford signalman waits to collect the Kirkby branch token from the driver of 142058 as he approaches the station on 9 May 2003 with a Kirkby–Rochdale service.

Below Right: 142053 prepares to stop at Newton-le-Willows on 29 December 2000 whilst working a Liverpool Lime St–Manchester Victoria service.

142042, from the second tranche of Merseyrail trainsets, is coupled to Class 156 156497 as they pass Selside on 29 December 2005 whilst working a Leeds–Carlisle service.

The Rainford signalman waits to collect the Kirkby branch token from the driver of 142043 as he approaches the station on 13 May 2003 with a Kirkby–Rochdale service.

142043 approaches Stockport on 17 August 2002 whilst working a Manchester Piccadilly–Chester service.

142048 departs from Southport on 10 September 2003 whilst working a Southport–Rochdale service.

142044 + Class 150/1 150147 call at Parbold on 4 May 2005 whilst working a Southport–Rochdale service.

142058 stands at Liverpool Lime St platform on 15 March 2006 awaiting its next turn of duty.

Left: 142049 drifts past Winwick on 28 October 2002 whilst working a Liverpool Lime St–Warrington Bank Quay service.

Below Left: 142051 calls at Edge Hill on 28 November 2003 whilst working a Liverpool Lime St–Manchester Victoria service.

Below Right: 142044 stands in Preston station on 11 March 2003 after its arrival with a Colne–Preston service.

3.3: Privatisation

British Railways was privatised under the Railways Act 1993 which became effective from 1 April 1994 when all rolling stock was distributed between Rolling Stock Companies (ROSCOs) who then hired it to the individual Train Operating Companies (TOCs). The consequence for the 'Pacer' fleet was that the Class 142 trainsets were passed to Angel Trains and the Class 143/144 trainsets passed to Porterbrook Leasing Company and these ROSCOs then became responsible for the hiring of 'Pacer' trainsets to the TOCs.

The structure of Regional Railways, as provider of local services, was also changed by being re-organised into four separate companies that formed the first tranche of franchises; these were Regional Railways North West (covering the north-west of England), Regional Railways North East (covering the north-east of England), Cardiff Valley Lines (covering the South Wales Valley lines in the Cardiff area) and South Wales and West (covering services in South Wales and the West Country).

While the Class 142 fleet was initially split between the North West and North East companies, post-privatisation moves saw class members being re-allocated to TOCs, later franchises, hence the sequence of franchises is given in this section, although reference to them will be made in the sections relating to Classes 143/144.

3.3.1: Regional Railways North West

The company continued operating as Regional Railways until the first franchise began on 2 March 1997 when First Group started operating as North Western Trains but changing its trading name to First North Western (FNW) in November 1998. It took some time to create a corporate livery hence in the meantime it simply branded existing trainsets with 'First North West' until the new livery was revealed. This first franchise lasted until 2004 when the second franchise was awarded to Serco-NedRailways which began operations as Northern Rail from 12 December 2004. The third franchise was awarded to Arriva Trains which retained the Northern trading name, albeit re-styled, and began operations from April 2016. A new livery was revealed in December 2016 but, as at March 2017, it has not been applied to the 'Pacer' fleet on the grounds that the franchise commitment includes the condition that the fleet must be replaced by 2019.

3.3.1.1: First North West (FNW) [2 March 1997 to 11 December 2004]

142067 + Class 150/1 150141 curve through Balshaw Lane Junction on 19 February 2000 whilst working a Liverpool Lime St–Blackpool North service. Of interest is that 142067 bears pre-franchise livery and FNW branding whilst 150141 bears the new FNW 'star' corporate livery and branding.

142029 curves through Winwick on 18 October 2002 whilst working a Liverpool Lime St–Warrington Bank Quay service.

142003 prepares to leave Preston on 17 May 2002 with a convoy to Blackpool North Carriage Sidings comprising 142067 and Class 153/0 153310.

142004 stables at Southport on 2 January 2001.

142039 calls at Bamber Bridge on 4 May 2002 whilst working a Blackpool South–Colne service.

142003 + Class 150/2 doyen 150201 speed through Salwick on 24 January 2001 whilst working a Blackpool North–Liverpool Lime St service.

142039 approaches Stockport on 17 August 2002 whilst working a Manchester Piccadilly–Chester service.

142029 calls at Leyland on 14 February 2002, still bearing GMPTE logo, whilst working a Liverpool Lime St–Lancaster service.

142044 bears revised Regional Railways Grey livery and FNW branding as it curves through Salwick on 10 June 2000 with a Colne–Blackpool South service.

142036 bears revised Regional Railways Grey livery and FNW branding as it calls at Leyland on 19 March 2002 whilst working Blackpool North–Liverpool Lime St service.

Resplendent in FNW blue livery with 'star' connectors, 142070 approaches Leyland on 10 June 2003 with a Liverpool Lime St–Blackpool North service.

142003 departs from Southport on 14 April 2004 whilst working a Southport–Rochdale service.

142023 passes Winwick on 18 October 2002 whilst working a Liverpool Lime St–Warrington Bank Quay service.

142035 departs from Manchester Piccadilly on 24 June 2003 whilst working a local service to Marple.

142023 prepares to depart from Wigan North Western on 15 July 2000 whilst working a Wigan North Western–Liverpool Lime St service.

The driver of 142034 collects the single line token for the Kirkby branch from the Rainford signalman on 31 March 2003 whilst working a Rochdale–Kirkby service.

Right: 142032 approaches Bamber Bridge on 3 August 2002 whilst working a Blackpool South–Colne service.

Below: An unidentified Class 142 trainset crosses the River Kent at Arnside on 14 October 2003 whilst working a Liverpool Lime St–Millom service.

3.3.1.2: Northern Rail (NR) [12 December 2004 to 31 March 2016]

The second franchise was awarded to Serco-NedRailways, a joint venture between Serco and NedRailways (a private company created by the Dutch National Railway company (NS = Nederlandse Spoorweg) to bid for railway contracts outside Holland). This franchise traded as 'Northern Rail' when it began operating on 12 December 2004 but it differed from the previous franchise in the following ways:

i.   the North Wales routes were transferred to the Wales & Borders franchise on 28 September 2003

ii. services to Barrow and Windermere were transferred to the Trans Pennine Express franchise on 1 February 2003

iii. the local services previously operated by Arriva Trains Northern were now included in the new franchise

As with the previous franchise changeover, the new company took time to create a corporate livery and branding during which time the rolling stock operated in its previous livery with either no branding or a temporary 'Northern' branding.

Class doyen 142001 bears unbranded FNW livery as it stables in Preston on 3 March 2005.

142005 bears unbranded FNW livery as it awaits departure from Blackpool South on 2 March 2005 whilst working a Blackpool South–Colne service.

Examples of trainsets bearing unbranded FNW livery.

Right: 142011 curves away from the WCML at Farington on 3 March 2005 whilst working a Blackpool South–Colne service.

Below Left: 142062 curves away from Hellifield on 18 February 2006 whilst working a Morecambe–Leeds service.

Below Right: 142039 approaches Squires Gate on 18 March 2005 whilst working a Blackpool South–Colne service.

142004 curves through an autumnal mist at Winwick on 7 December 2004 whilst working a Warrington Bank Quay–Liverpool Lime St service.

A trio of FNW liveried trainsets with temporary 'Northern' branding sees:

142027 departing from Manchester Piccadilly on 5 January 2006 en route to Longsight depot for servicing.

142061 curving through Oubeck on 2 November 2006 with a Liverpool Lime St–Morecambe service.

142060 calling at Salford Crescent on 5 January 2006 with a Wigan Wallgate–Rochdale service.

The new corporate livery was introduced after trials with various liveries carried by Class 156 trainsets and is seen to good effect on 142037 as it is 'panned' crossing the Moss at Martin's Lane on 16 January 2012 whilst working a Southport–Manchester Victoria service.

Scenes at Preston station

Class doyen 142001 enters the station on 22 January 2014 whilst working a Colne–Blackpool South service.

142004 approaches the bay platform on 25 July 2012 whilst working an Ormskirk–Preston shuttle service.

142048 approaches the station on 13 July 2012 whilst working a Colne–Blackpool South service.

142049 approaches the bay platform on 24 July 2012 whilst working an Ormskirk–Preston shuttle service.

142049 stands at Ormskirk 'interchange' on 10 April 2013 as Class 507 trainset 507033 *Councillor Jack Spriggs* waits to continue to Liverpool; the once through line is now divided by a buffer stop between the two trainsets that is seen in front of 142049.

Scenes at Southport

142054 + Class 150/1 150136 curve through St Lukes on 2 May 2011 whilst working a Wigan Wallgate–Southport service.

142035 + 142060 enter the station on 2 May 2011 whilst working an empty stock service from Wigan Wallgate Carriage Sidings to Southport

142060 + 142035 curve through the station approach on 2 May 2011 whilst working an empty stock move from Wigan Wallgate Carriage Sidings to Southport.

142048 + 142056 curve through the approach to St Lukes on 29 May 2013 whilst working a Southport–Manchester Airport service.

142052 approaches the station on 31 March 2012 whilst working a Manchester Airport–Southport service.

Scenes from the Southport–Wigan Line

142084 + 142013 approach Burscough Bridge on 15 May 2012 whilst working a Southport–Manchester Airport service.

142057 speeds through Bescar Lane on 7 November 2011 whilst working a Manchester Airport–Southport service.

142046 speeds through the staggered platforms at Bescar Lane on 7 November 2011 whilst working a Southport–Manchester Victoria service.

142048 + 142056 curve through St Lukes on 29 May 2013 whilst working a Manchester Victoria–Southport service.

142031 speeds past the staggered platforms at New Lane on 2 November 2007 whilst working a Southport–Rochdale service.

Left: 142055 calls at Salwick on 26 January 2011 whilst working a Colne–Blackpool South service.

Above: 142035 + Class 150/2 150205 breast Hoghton summit on 11 August 2013 whilst working a Blackpool North–York service as substitute for the normal Class 158 traction.

Below: 142052 races through Balshaw Lane Junction on 8 June 2011 whilst working a Liverpool Lime St–Blackpool North service.

Left: 142042 + 142045 draw away from Buckshaw Parkway on 21 August 2012 after calling with a Hazel Grove–Preston service.

Below Left: 142061 draws away from Bamber Bridge on 20 July 2011 whilst working a Blackpool South–Colne service.

Below Right: 142079 + Class 150/1 150138 draw away from Buckshaw Parkway on 14 July 2013 whilst working a Manchester Victoria–Blackpool North service.

Scenes from Manchester Oxford Road – This Page

Right: 142047 curves into the bay platform on 4 February 2010 whilst working a service from Liverpool Lime St.

Below Left: 142051 + 142055 call at nearby Deansgate on 4 February 2000 whilst working a Liverpool Lime St–Manchester Oxford Road service.

Below Right: 142055 + 142056 approach on 3 July 2013 whilst working a Southport–Manchester Airport service.

Scenes from Winwick – Opposite Page

Top Left: 142087 passes on 14 March 2012 whilst working a Warrington Bank Quay–Liverpool Lime St service.

Top Right: 142028 passes on 27 March 2015 with a Warrington Bank Quay–Liverpool Lime St service.

Below Left: 142053 passes on 6 April 2011 with a Warrington Bank Quay–Liverpool Lime St service.

Below Right: 142055 passes on 24 February 2011 whilst working a Warrington Bank Quay–Liverpool Lime St service.

Opposite Page

Top Left: 142012 forms the rear of a Preston–Hazel Grove service awaiting departure from Preston on 1 May 2013.

Top Right: 142047 passes Euxton Balshaw Lane on 16 August 2013 whilst working a Preston–Manchester Victoria empty stock service.

Below Left: 142051 + 142056 call at Salford Crescent on 12 December 2013 whilst working a Manchester Airport–Southport service.

Below Right: 142049 joins the WCML at Winwick Junction on 15 April 2011 whilst working a Liverpool Lime St–Warrington Bank Quay service.

This Page

Right: 142013 forms the rear of a Southport–Manchester Airport service led by 142084 as it calls at Burscough Bridge on 15 May 2012.

Below Left: 142092 calls at Bamber Bridge on 11 July 2012 whilst working a Colne–Blackpool South service.

Below Right: 142060 calls at Shaw and Crompton on 1 October 2009 whilst working a Rochdale–Manchester Victoria service during the last week of 'heavy' rail operation.

Right: 142039 approaches Edale on 20 March 2010 whilst working a Manchester Piccadilly–Sheffield service.

Below Left: 142093 forms the rear of a Leeds–Manchester Victoria service led by Class 158/9 158910 William Wilberforce as they call at Hebden Bridge on 30 October 2012.

Below Right: 142096 + 142071 weave out of Doncaster on 19 January 2017 whilst working a Scunthorpe–Lincoln service.

Scenes from Copmanthorpe on the southern outskirts of York

Right: 142067 passes on 16 April 2014 whilst working a York–Hull service.

Below Left: 142095 passes on 16 November 2011 whilst working a York–Sheffield service.

Below Right: 142020 passes on 16 April 2014 whilst working a York–Sheffield service.

142067 + 142057 await departure from Southport on 2 May 2011 whilst working a Southport–Wigan Wallgate CS stock move.

142062 is stabled at Liverpool Lime St at the end of the day on 23 October 2012.

142045 + 142036 are stabled at Southport on 1 January 2013.

142056 is stabled at Manchester Piccadilly on 19 January 2012.

142049 calls at Preston on 13 February 2011 whilst working a Blackpool South–Colne service.

Right: 142023 awaits departure from Burscough Bridge on 22 July 2007 whilst working an Alderley Edge–Southport service.

Below: 142050 speeds through Hest Bank on 20 August 2014 whilst working a Lancaster–Leeds service. Of interest is that this trainset was trialled from new with the Voith hydraulic transmission that subsequently replaced the SCG transmission on all 'Pacer' trainsets.

Right: 142090 passes the NRM's Shildon site on 7 October 2011 whilst working a Bishop Auckland–Darlington service.

3.3.1.3: Northern Railways (NR) [1 April 2016 to 31 March 2025]

This third franchise was awarded to Arriva Trains North (ATN), trading as Northern Railways (NR), in December 2015 and began on 1 April 2016 albeit with yet a different area of operation from the previous one.

i. services to Barrow and Windermere were returned from the Trans Pennine Express franchise, including the stations served by the trains
ii. the local service between Cleethorpes and Barton on Humber will transfer to the East Midlands Trains franchise in October 2017.

ATN elected to retain the 'Northern' branding but with a revised logo and livery which was introduced from December 2016. The 'Pacer' fleet is due to be withdrawn during this franchise hence trainsets have retained the livery of the previous franchisee but with the branding removed. As at December 2016 there are no indications that any branding will be displayed on 'Pacer' trainsets operated by this franchisee.

142051 + 142017 pass Euxton on 1 October 2016 whilst working a Blackpool North–Manchester Victoria service.

142001 curves through Lostock Hall on 9 June 2016 whilst working a Blackpool South–Colne service.

142029 + 142040 approach Preston on 23 November 2016 whilst working a Manchester Victoria–Blackpool North service.

142034 stands at Preston on 7 May 2016 as part of a consist forming a Preston–Blackpool North CS stock move for overnight servicing.

142061 + Class 156 156461 call at Manchester Piccadilly in the early hours of 19 January 2017 whilst working a Southport–Manchester Airport service.

142040 approaches Preston on 22 November 2016 whilst working a Colne–Blackpool South service.

3.3.2: Regional Railways North East

The company continued operating as Regional Railways until the first franchise began on 2 March 1997 when MTL, a company created by MerseyTravel to secure rail franchises, was awarded the franchise that began on 2 March 1997. The company ran into trouble by 2000 and in February 2000 sold its interest to Arriva Trains who subsequently traded as Arriva Trains Northern (ATN). The Strategic Rail Authority restructured the franchise in 2004, with the express services becoming part of the new Trans Pennine Express franchise and the local services becoming part of the Northern Rail franchise (see 3.3.1.2).

3.3.2.1: Northern Spirit (NS) [2 March 1997 to 17 February 2000]

MTL operated its services as Northern Spirit (NS) and when it first began operating, it concentrated on re-branding the express trainsets leaving the 'Pacer' fleet, based between Leeds Neville Hill and Heaton depots, to bear the Regional Railways Grey livery that all its Class 142 units then bore. When replaced by ATN, only five units had received the NS corporate livery and branding hence ATN immediately branded all units with 'ARRIVA' branding until this could subsequently be replaced by the Arriva corporate bus livery of blue body with white flash.

142050 carries full Northern Spirit local livery and branding on 12 February 2001 as it passes Hambleton North whilst working a York–Goole service.

3.3.2.2: Arriva Trains North (ATN) [18 February 2000 to 11 December 2004]

The Northern Spirit franchise quickly became a loss-maker and MTL sold out its railway interests to Arriva Trains North (ATN) which took over the franchise from 18 February 2000, although re-branding of its trains did not begin until 27 April 2001. At that time the fleet included 28 Class 142 'Pacer' trainsets; 17 in Regional Railways Grey livery; 6 in Tyne & Wear Metro Yellow livery and 5 repainted into NS local livery.

The franchise continued until 11 December 2004 when it was merged with parts of the First North Western (FNW) franchise to create the Northern Rail franchise that began operating from 12 December 2004 (see 3.3.1.2) – and where further examples of the Class 142 'Pacer' fleet can be viewed.

Right: 142091 bears unbranded Regional Railways Grey livery as it passes Billingham whilst working a Middlesbrough–Hexham service on 5 November 2003; two days earlier …

Below Left: 142024, bearing Arriva branding, crosses the viaduct at Chester-le-Street on 7 November 2003 whilst working a Saltburn–Newcastle service.

Below Right: 142091 departing from Darlington Bank Top whilst working a local service to Saltburn.

Left: 142022 bears Tyne & Wear Metro Yellow livery as it calls at Chester-le-Street on 6 November 2003 whilst working a Saltburn–Newcastle service. This trainset was one of six (142017–022) to carry this livery which was originally applied to Class 143 143020–025 (see Section 4); when the latter were transferred to Cardiff in 1991, the livery was applied to the Class 142 units to denote the continuing Tyne & Wear sponsorship of local Metro services.

Below Left: 142065 bears unbranded Northern Spirit livery as it climbs away from Hellifield on 13 October 2005 whilst working a Morecambe–Leeds service.

Below Right: 142084 bears Arriva branding on its Regional Railways Grey livery as it stands in York on 2 December 2003 awaiting its next duty.

Northern Spirit liveried units which bore Arriva branding included:

Left: 142050 calling at Newcastle on 26 May 2004 whilst working a Metro Centre–Morpeth service.

Above: 142025 + Class 156 156484 approaching Dewsbury on 15 June 2004 whilst working a Leeds–Huddersfield service.

Below: 142066 calling at St Peters on 26 May 2004 whilst working a Hexham–Sunderland service.

ATN's corporate blue livery with white flash was quickly introduced and carried by:

Opposite page

142079 approaching Blaydon on 27 May 2004 whilst working a Hexham–Sunderland service.

This page

Top Right: 142016 approaching Hexham on 25 May 2004 whilst working a Middlesbrough–Carlisle service.

Below Left: 142078 approaching Newcastle on 12 March 2004 whilst working a Middlesbrough–Hexham service.

Below Right: 142021 entering Newcastle on 11 March 2004 whilst working a Saltburn–Newcastle service.

Trainsets retaining unbranded ATN livery whilst working services operated by successor Northern Rail franchise which began on 12 December 2004 (see 3.3.1.2) included:

Opposite page

Far Left: 142094 curving into Hellifield on 15 November 2005 whilst working a Morecambe–Leeds service.

Top Right: 142019 passing Euxton Junction on 24 March 2007 whilst working a Blackpool North–Liverpool Lime St service.

Bottom Right: 142071 weaving out of Doncaster on 3 June 2005 whilst working a Scunthorpe–Sheffield service.

This page

Right: 142096 stabling in Southport on 10 July 2009 whilst awaiting its next duty.

Below: 142079 climbing away from Hellifield on 17 February 2006 whilst working a Leeds–Morecambe service.

3.3.3: Valley Lines

The Valley Line network was initially a stand-alone franchise that was awarded to Prism Rail which began trading as Valley Lines from October 1996 to run to October 2001; in October 2000 the company was bought by National Express who continued with the franchise unchanged. In 1998/9 the company exchanged 10 of its Class 150/2 trainsets (150268–277) for 11 Class 142 Pacers from Neville Hill (142085 – 094; 142096); the latter trainsets were quickly given Valley Lines livery.

The franchise was subject to change in 2000 when the Strategic Rail Authority (SRA) combined the Valley Lines franchise with the Wales and West franchise to create two new franchises – Wales & Borders Railway to provide services in South Wales, and Wessex Trains to provide services in the West Country; both franchises started operating in October 2001. The Wales & Border franchise was subsequently re-tendered and in August 2001 was awarded to the Arriva Group which began operating services as Arriva Trains Wales (ATW) from December 2003.

3.3.3.1: Arriva Trains Wales (ATW) [8 December 2003 to 31 March 2018]

Opposite page

142010 approaches Pontypridd on 27 February 2004 whilst working a Treherbert–Barry Island service.

This page

Left: 142076 leaves Barry Island on 27 February 2004 whilst working a Barry Island–Caerphilly service.

Below Left: A comparison of liveries at Rhymney on 7 July 2005 as 142080 *Caerphilly RF* in Arriva-branded Valley Lines livery + 142002 in Arriva corporate blue livery with white flash depart from Rhymney with a service to Penarth.

Below Right: 142074 calls at Barry on 7 July 2005 whilst working a Caerphilly–Bridgend service.

142075 bears Arriva corporate blue livery with white flash as it stables in Rhymney Sidings on 4 December 2005 in the company of Class 150/2 150280.

142069 crosses Porthkerry Viaduct on 4 July 2005 whilst working a Bridgend–Caerphilly service.

Far from its normal area of operation, 142069 carries unbranded Valley Lines livery as it departs from Kirkham on 5 February 2004 whilst working a Colne–Blackpool South service.

142002 + 142080 *Caerphilly RFC* depart from Rhymney on 7 July 2005 whilst working a Rhymney–Penarth service.

Section 4:
Class 143

The Class 143 trainsets were ordered from Hunslet-Barclay with bodies supplied by Walter Alexander and delivered to Provincial Railways' Heaton depot for services in the North East of England based around Newcastle, Sunderland and Middlesbrough. Trainsets 143001–019 were delivered in the Provincial Railways two-tone blue livery whilst the final six, 143020–143025, were delivered in the Tyne and Wear Yellow livery following their purchase of the vehicles for Tyne & Wear services. Shortly after delivery some sets were loaned to Haymarket depot to operate services on the newly-opened Edinburgh–Bathgate line as a temporary measure until a tranche of Class 150/2 trainsets could be obtained as a permanent measure.

In 1989 the decision was taken to replace both engines and transmissions of the 'Pacer' fleet with Class 143 units being the first to undergo modification and receive the new fleet numbers that had been specified to differentiate between original and modified trainsets. In the case of Class 143 trainsets this involved changing the 0xx serial numbers to 6xx; the new serial numbers were retained despite the policy changing shortly after and subsequent modified 'Pacer' trainsets retaining their original serial numbers.

The extending Tyne & Wear Metro network took over many local services which released the Class 143 trainsets and allowed their transfer to Cardiff during 1991/92 where they took over local services, including those of the Cardiff Valley network. When BR was privatised in 1994 the fleet was split between the two local franchises – the Valley Lines and the South Wales & West Railway – which began operating in October 1996.

The trainsets had all received the Regional Railways Grey livery but the Valley Lines quickly adopted a new livery that was continued when the Strategic Rail Authority (SRA) restructured the franchises in 2000. It combined the Valley Lines and the South Wales & West Railway to create the Wales & Border Railway, based at Cardiff, to service local trains in South Wales and Wessex Trains, based at Bristol, to service local trains in the West Country; these new franchises began to operate from October 2001. The Wales & Border Railway franchise was awarded to Arriva Group in September 2003 and began operating as Arriva Trains Wales (ATW) from December 2005. The SRA then turned to restructure the Great Western franchise in 2002 by combining it with the Thames Valley and Wessex Trains franchise to create a Greater Western franchise which was awarded to First Group in December 2005 and began operating from April 2006.

Of interest is that, as at December 2016, trainsets 143601/10/14 are owned by Mid-Glamorgan County Council, 143613 is owned by South Glamorgan County Council and 143617–19 are owned by First Greater Western although all units are managed by the Porterbrook Leasing Company.

4.1: Provincial Railways *[1982 to 3 April 1989] later Regional Railways [4 April 1989 to 31 March 1997]*

143613 awaits departure from Battersby on 15 September 1989 whilst working a Whitby–Middlesbrough service; at the rear 143614 + Class 142 142519, bearing the GWR-style chocolate and cream 'Skipper' livery, await departure for Whitby with a Middlesbrough–Whitby service.

143015 + 143010 curve into Grosmont on 17 April 1987 whilst working a Whitby–Middlesbrough service.

143022, bearing Tyne & Wear Metro livery, departs from Grosmont on 17 April 1987 whilst working a Middlesbrough–Whitby service.

143005 + 143017 await departure from Windermere on 8 August 1991 whilst working a Windermere–Oxenholme service.

143625, bearing Tyne & Wear Metro livery, approaches Staveley on 28 February 1992 whilst working an Oxenholme–Windermere service.

4.2: Arriva Trains Wales [8 December 2003 to 31 March 2018]

When a rugby game is played at Cardiff's Millennium Stadium, the local transport arrangements include the provision of rail shuttle services between Newport and Cardiff using all available trainsets from local 'Pacer' trainsets to Inter City HSTs. On 29 February 2004 one such shuttle service was operated by 143601 + 143608, here seen passing Coed Kernow as empty stock en route to Newport to collect more passengers for Cardiff.

143616 curves into Pontypridd on 27 February 2004 whilst working a Treherbert–Barry Island service.

143624 calls at Taffs Well on 27 February 2004 whilst working a Pontypridd–Caerphilly service.

143604 awaits departure from Merthyr with a service to Penarth on 27 February 2004.

143625 approaches Gilfach on 7 July 2005 whilst working a Cardiff–Rhymney service.

Left: 143618 approaches Nailsea on 26 October 2004 whilst working a Bristol Temple Meads–Weston Super Mare service.

Right: 143617 approaches Stroud on 24 September 2004 whilst working a Swindon–Cheltenham service.

143613 stables with a sister unit in Gloucester station yard on 24 September 2004 whilst awaiting its next duty.

When a rugby game is played at Cardiff's Millennium Stadium, the local transport arrangements include the provision of rail shuttle services between Newport and Cardiff using all available trainsets from local 'Pacer' trainsets to Inter City HSTs. On 29 February 2004 one such shuttle service was operated by 143620 + 143617 + 143619, here seen passing Coed Kernow as empty stock en route to Newport to collect more passengers for Cardiff.

4.4: First Great Western [FGW] *[1 April 2006 to 31 March 2019]* later re-branded Great Western Railways [GWR] *[20 September 2015 to 31 March 2019]*

The Wessex Trains Class 143 trainsets became part of the First Great Western fleet hence were transferred to Exeter for use on local services where they were subsequently re-liveried in FGW local livery. One local working is the Exmouth–Paignton service which was noted at Dawlish on 26 August 2016 when:

Right: shortly after returned with 143612 leading on a Paignton–Exmouth service.

Below: 143612 was coupled to Class 153/1 153369 as they passed Dawlish with an Exmouth–Paignton service.

Section 5:
Class 144

The Class 144 trainsets were ordered from British Rail Engineering Ltd (BREL) Derby Works with bodies supplied by Walter Alexander and delivered to Provincial Railways' Neville Hill depot during 1986/7. They were intended for local services sponsored by the West Yorkshire Passenger Transport Executive (WYPTE) hence supplied bearing the WYPTE red/buttermilk livery. In 1987 WYPTE ordered a further ten motor trailer vehicles that converted trainsets 144014–23 to 3-car trainsets.

When BR was privatised the units passed to Regional Railways North East but retained WYPTE livery and were managed by Porterbrook Leasing; three units,

144011–13, had received Regional Railways Grey livery in 1994, but the remainder retained the WYPTE livery until Arriva Trains Northern (ATN) took over the franchise in 2000. Refurbishment of the trainsets began in 2002 and included a revised livery with Metro branding but, when the franchise passed to Northern Rail in December 2004, they were re-liveried in that company's livery with only the Metro branding remaining to identify the WYPTE sponsorship of services around the Leeds/Sheffield area.

5.1: Provincial Railways [1982 to 3 April 1989]

144022, operating in 3-car formation and bearing original WYPTE livery, calls at Appleby on 30 April 1994 whilst working a Carlisle–Leeds service.

5.2: Regional Railways *[4 April 1989 to 1 March 1997]*

Right: 144011, one of three trainsets to receive Regional Railways Grey livery and branding, curves past Burton Salmon on 11 June 1996 whilst working a York–Sheffield service.

Below Right: 144015 ambles past Morecambe Lodge on 30 May 1996 whilst nearing Lancaster with a Leeds–Morecambe service.

Below Left: 144010 + Class 158/9 158903 curve through Farington Moss on 10 March 1995 whilst working a Blackpool North–York service.

Right: 144014 curves away from Ben Rhydding on 10 March 1995 whilst working an Ilkley–Leeds service.

Below Left: 144006 is at the rear of a Carlisle–Leeds service led by Class 156 156498 as they prepare to leave Appleby on 1 June 1996.

Below Right: 144017 approaches Steeton on 10 March 1995 whilst working a Skipton–Bradford service.

144001 races past Steeton on 10 March 1995 whilst working a Bradford–Skipton service.

144017 awaits departure from Skipton on 10 March 1995 whilst working a Skipton–Bradford service.

144022 departs from Ilkley on 13 June 2000 whilst working an Ilkley–Bradford service.

5.3: Merseyside Travel Ltd (MTL) *[2 March 1997 to 17 February 2000]*

MTL concentrated on the development of its Trans Pennine services and only five Pacer trainsets of Class 142 received the corporate 'Northern Spirit' livery. One of the three Class 144 trainsets that received the Regional Railways Grey livery was noted after this franchise was sold to Arriva Trains North (ATN) but before receiving Arriva's corporate 'Metro' livery; 144012 was noted at Lancaster as it reversed direction on 9 June 2001 whilst working a Leeds–Morecambe service.

5.4: Arriva Trains North *[17 February 2000 to 11 December 2004]*

The New Order

Left: 144014 stands at Starbeck on 1 December 2003 whilst working a Leeds–Knaresborough service.

Below: 144001 *The Penistone Line Partnership* calls at Wakefield Westgate on 3 December 2003 whilst working a Leeds–Sheffield service.

The Old Order

Opposite page: 144016 curves through the approach to Whitby on 4 November 2003 whilst working a Middlesbrough–Whitby service. The use of a 3-car trainset was required to meet the demand for school travel from Esk Valley locations to Whitby.–

144022 calls at Sleights on
3 November 2003 whilst working
a Whitby–Middlesbrough service.

144012 stands at Lancaster on 29 October 2004 whilst awaiting departure with a Morecambe–Leeds service.

144003 approaches Starbeck on 1 December 2003 whilst working a York–Leeds service

111

144006 carries 'Northern' branding as it curves through Eldroth on 5 February 2009 whilst working a Morecambe–Leeds service.

5.5: Northern Rail (NR) *[12 December 2004 to 31 March 2016]*

144014 carries no Train Operating Company (TOC) branding as it calls at Preston on 5 February 2005 whilst working a York–Blackpool North service.

144011 carries 'Northern' branding as it weaves out of Lancaster on 6 June 2007 whilst working a Leeds–Morecambe service.

144009, bearing temporary 'Northern' branding, curves out of Hellifield on 5 May 2003 whilst working a Morecambe–Leeds service.

144018, bearing temporary 'Northern' branding and revised 'Metro' branding curves out of Hellifield on 27 March 2007 whilst working a Morecambe–Leeds service.

144022 bears the 'Northern Rail' corporate livery and 'Metro' branding as it curves through Hest Bank on 11 April 2015 whilst working a Morecambe–Leeds service.

Scenes from the Calder Valley

144018 passes Eastwood on 8 June 2011 whilst working a Leeds–Manchester Victoria service.

144003 passes Eastwood on 17 July 2010 whilst working a Manchester Victoria–Selby service.

144021 calls at Hebden Bridge on 30 October 2012 with a Hebden Bridge–Leeds service.

Right: 144005 + 144002 call at Doncaster on 23 October 2014 whilst working a Lincoln–Scunthorpe service.

Below Left: 144021 is stabled in Sheffield station on 1 November 2015.

Below Right: 144008 calls at Rochdale on 1 September 2008 whilst working a Manchester Victoria–Leeds service.

The 'Pacer' fleets are being withdrawn from service by 31 December 2019 because the trainsets do not meet the Rail Vehicle Accessibility (Interoperable Rail System) Regulations 2008 for 'persons with reduced mobility' but, in 2015, Porterbrook Leasing Company upgraded 144012 to meet the latest requirements. The trainset was classified Class 144e (for 'evolution') and released in 2015 as a 'demonstrator' trainset, fitted with a fully accessible toilet, two wheelchair spaces and additional spaces for bicycles and luggage.

Right: View of the vehicle entrance when stabled in Sheffield station on 1 November 2015.

Below: View of the trainset when stabled in Sheffield station on 1 November 2015.

Class 144e 'demonstrator' trainset 144012 weaves out of Doncaster on 7 January 2017 whilst working a Scunthorpe–Lincoln service.